ESCAPE GIRL BLUES

poems by

Dawn Pichón Barron

Finishing Line Press
Georgetown, Kentucky

ESCAPE GIRL BLUES

Copyright © 2018 by Dawn Pichón Barron
ISBN 978-1-63534-392-2 First Edition
All rights reserved under International and Pan-American Copyright Conventions. No part of this book may be reproduced in any manner whatsoever without written permission from the publisher, except in the case of brief quotations embodied in critical articles and reviews.

ACKNOWLEDGMENTS

I am grateful to the following journals for bringing my work to the light. Yakoke, Muchas Gracias, & Heartfelt Thank you:

Pontoon, 2017 "UNDER THE BRIDGE"
Washington 129 Anthology, 2017 "LUCKY"
Pittsburgh Poetry Review, 2017 "ONE WAY BACK," "ESCAPE GIRL BLUES," "TO LIE OR LAY"
Yellow Medicine Review, 2016 "COWBOYS & INDIAN PRINCESSES"

Publisher: Leah Maines
Editor: Christen Kincaid
Cover Art: Daniel Barron
Author Photo: Cortney Kelley Photography
Cover Design: Elizabeth Maines McCleavy

Printed in the USA on acid-free paper.
Order online: www.finishinglinepress.com
also available on amazon.com

Author inquiries and mail orders:
Finishing Line Press
P. O. Box 1626
Georgetown, Kentucky 40324
U. S. A.

Table of Contents

DARK MATTER 1
TO LIE OR LAY 2
SKIN PICKLED 4
UNDER THE BRIDGE 5
A LITTLE LESS CONVERSATION 6
MIXING HISTORY FOR DANIEL 7
MAN CAMPS 8
TRUTH 9
IT DOESN'T HAVE TO MATTER 10
CHAIN-SMOKING AT STANDING
    BEAR'S GRAVESITE 12
LUCKY 13
AMERICAN CRUSADE 14
BENDING, BENDING 15
EPISTEMOLOGIES & NO APOLOGIES 16
ONE WAY BACK 17
WE ARE ALL FATED 18
TRUTH 19
JUAN DIEGO'S ONE EYE 20
SEWN TIGHT 21
COWBOYS & INDIAN PRINCESSES 22
BOCA GRANDE 24
THE RED DRESS FLATTENS ME 25
ESCAPE GIRL BLUES 26
WOMEN BE WISE 27

For my wingman—*siempre,* my love spawns,
& *mi familia:* past, present, & future.

Prefiero morir de pie que vivir de rodillas.
~Emiliano Zapato Salazar

That is all, the drunkenness of life, the stirring and crawling of the yeast,...
~Jack London, The Sea-Wolf

DARK MATTER

I want to tell you a story by
Telling you nothing

& inside that is this dark matter we once thought nothing &
like nothing we didn't realize until it became something
we are all fish in water at the very moment fish know
water to be water

From me to you
        Used to be nothing but space, vacant & empty
& now it isn't true

Beauty of Truth.

TO LIE OR LAY

I.
While slinking through childhood
Trying to please and learn how to stuff
All that stuff that doesn't feel right
Not knowing how to lie, yet lying
I ate that dog shit knowing it didn't feel right
Looking away from the older kids who promised
Bags of candy   and to tell on me
So I ate dog shit and didn't cry
Because they told me not to

II.
Animals don't lie and this makes them lovable
Easy to hurt even if it doesn't feel right
When our dad took us for a ride
In the wood-paneled station wagon
Crowded and scared, April looked at me
I tasted dog shit as she
Fought the rope leading to   slaughter
I prayed for our pet goat and didn't cry
Because he told me not to

III.
The animal in all us lies wait
You are a girl and it doesn't feel right
Choke down that Everclear, put your lips around what is offered
Smile like you know what you are doing
Until you don't   wake up bloodied
The girl now woman body
Feels butchered, carved, swollen beyond
You (and I) forget not to cry
Because nobody is awake to tell you not to

IV.
Lying becomes a natural border
Invisible wall that feels almost right
If right feels like safety and some sort of untouchable
Or like being other/else/non-self
The child in you long destroyed now
It must be you
If it doesn't feel right
Because who eats dog shit and their pet goat   without crying

SKIN PICKLED

Bumps and wrinkles no different color than before
'Cept more transparent, waxy
Remember collecting autumn leaves,
Placing between wax paper and coloring
To capture the veins, the shape
Too long in the bath renders me a wax paper
Self. A deconstruction without taking apart.
Afraid to get out, slip and crack open
A piece, some important part of me.
Always have blue painter's tape around;
Won't leave a lasting mark but pulls the pieces
Together. 'Cept you become ironic
In a certain light. Courage only gets us so far
Or black-listed
Or killed.

UNDER THE BRIDGE

Hey Pocahontas, why don't you blow me with that mouth?
Hand travels to hair, loose. No braids.
Tug the wife-beater lifted from brother over the band of cut-offs.

He looks older. Unknown, unseen before now
Under the bridge where we hide, drink, smoke, fuck.
He moves closer, squats, thigh muscles bulge.

Once on the pillars, near the top, with the drum of traffic
Ain't nowhere to go but the river. Down.
Po-ca-hon-tas, he sing-songs.

Never done an Indian girl.
What time you have to be back at your tipi?
Done. Indian. Girl.

Hands a Big Gulp over. Sip through the red straw.
Throat burning. Haven't eaten all day and
The sun is setting; the sky a rotting peach.

A LITTLE LESS CONVERSATION

As the ear can only bend so long

& now I'm driving rage into your ivory teeth
Rowed & straight, weak by perfection

Call it poaching except you're on my land

& I'm the wild one, on hands and knees
Closer to strong, heart in mouth

MIXING HISTORY FOR DANIEL

He tells me
Not often, yet enough:
You've got a chip on your shoulder

He tells me, and I pretend listen
Fingering ache splaying across my skull
Rising above myself like a plume of volcanic ash
Pushing my skin taut with untiring apology
A chip the size of a 40 carat diamond
Raw/cloudy/sharp
Your tools find no success
No wizard tongue pressing, stretching me
Toward peace, not now, not ever?
You want me to brush it off
Ground it back into the earth
With my bare feet, mix new blood with old
As your deep ancestors sailed to
Here there be monsters
Mine fighting the monsters here

Leaving a trail of ashen tears

MAN CAMPS

> "It's growing faster than any place else in the country," the mayor said with a smile. "It's exciting. It's amazing what oil can do for you. Black Gold." ~Aljazeera.com "The dark side of the oil boom: Human trafficking in the heartland" by Aaron Ernst

Williston, I beg you to be a woman
To understand the breaking of hearts
And children. You are not; and I grieve
Oiled human tears for
How could you not know what would happen
With all those men? Men have not civilized
Themselves when they have drugs, alcohol,
Money to burn, anger to churn and seek
Release. Release, you know:
Hitting something, hurting something, fucking something
Turns out that something is a someone. A girl, a boy,
A woman. Yours, his, mine ours.
Bakken, a shale rock formation, now run through
By greed and gluttony. To be used, discarded, and
Folded into a burned memory. And when the Black Gold
Is gone, the shame will follow you; the broken will be left
Behind to fossilize their grief.

TRUTH

Did you know I was afraid of the dark?
Slept with a pillow over my head
Shoes on, ready to run

'Til I was twenty-three.

IT DOESN'T HAVE TO MATTER

My baby brother tells me this
I can't recall what we were talking about
Or if it was me lecturing
Half-mother, half-sister
To this now man I cannot place
As the smiling, swamp-eyed child who slept
In my bed, let me curl his hair, paint his nails
Pretend I had a sister
The bounced out of a truck bed on the highway kid
Not a bone broken, but we don't know
When the soft parts of us break
Not like the egg baby from Home Ec whose split
Guts we scooped up and flushed down the toilet
As if it never existed
A failed experiment
Like how I couldn't shelter my baby brother
From men with beer-breath and piss-yellow fingertips
Or from feeling trashed and dream spent
Later, part of me too proud when he learned to find his way with fists and
I struggled to hold then swallow the tiny spark of ignominy
While wishing whatever problem to walk away, and at the same time wanting
To see his lip split in two, nose cracked to the side

As an adult, a professional, tax paying wife and mother
Now even, I cannot settle on a definitive
As I teach my own that it does have to matter
Actions define us, exemptions may not apply

I give this nonetheless:
There are two types in the world
Those who avoid harm by retreat
Like hiding
Like running
Like silence
And those who avoid harm by attack
Like words
Like fists
Like guns
And to protect our own, logic doesn't have to matter.

CHAIN-SMOKING AT STANDING BEAR'S GRAVESITE

Dare to leave without offering a slice of your soul
They will hunt you down as you once hunted

Without proof you are human
As you walk like them, feet touching the land

The only thump they feel is the whack of your head
Not the beat of your heart, ferocious and fearful
Same as theirs, same as theirs

Stepping across the trip-line carrying your whole soul
Not shamed to tell who you are, a human being

Without knowing the highest Court may well tell you
Caged inside with your kind is where you belong

Personhood becomes another way to capture
The hatred that burrows deep within the same river
Of blood, same pile of bones lost

LUCKY

Years ago when given my first and only *escapulario*, the thin string around my neck holding a miniature cloth picture of the mother of all, the Mexican woman down the street told me to tuck it beneath my shirt—keep it pressed to my skin for protection. *Everyone like us must wear one*, she whispered.

Family Polaroids: three boys with dirty blonde hair and pale limbs surrounding a girl with eyes and hair the color of mud and skin, a stick of cinnamon.

In the rural outskirts of a northwestern town, a school official knocked on the front door, holding a free lunch form. Asked if my name meant Sun Rising, if I was adopted.

Every Halloween friends told me to be Pocahontas. With my beauty mark, I chose Gypsy. Once, I was a ghost.

During junior high, I moved to shaded areas, avoiding the greasy bottles of Baby Oil as others slathered and placed tinfoil reflectors on their pale bellies.

In high school, the Driver's Ed teacher snapped the seatbelt across my chest; *Bet you're a feisty one with that dark skin*. He scheduled my drives alone—so I could get more practice he said.

As a young adult, sitting across from a man I just met who had the same hair, eyes, and skin as me, I remembered my mom telling me, *You just tan real good, so count yourself lucky*.

Away at college, my best friend complimented me: *You almost look like a white girl…just with brown skin*.

A boyfriend, hands caressing my bare skin, murmured how he loved the color of me: *café con leche*, madrone bark, his little chestnut. I brushed his hands away. Feeling ghost.

AMERICAN CRUSADE

Limpieza de sangre "cleanliness of blood" traveled well-fed across an ocean, the mass graves and bone mountains a pure sign as eradication became best practice; and even today, the collective we have forgotten, or chosen the path of least resistance, conveniently misplacing our histories, as if the Crusades are not relevant; as if we are not still in *modus operandi*.

BENDING, BENDING

Pause button exists
On a world beyond
My hungry finger

I'm carried wild
On a raging cat
From heart poachers

To a dusty arroyo
Polishing my rib bones
To a bleached crimson

Wear my disappearing Indian
Like a threadbare coat
Trace the stars planted

Along my invisible map
Numbing the spin cycle
As each claim is staked

EPISTEMOLOGIES & NO APOLOGIES

You are sick to death of white privilege being thrown around
You say to a black man and red-brown woman
Putting back a couple of whiskeys, waiting for the band to play
Your arms are open wide, not crossed over
For being white and a man,
You are not remotely considering backlash,
Or a fist to your chest
You do not protect that heart of yours
It has never stopped beating or broke
The way a black man and red-brown woman
Have experienced—are expecting
You have no fear in the way you lean back, throat stretched
1 or 3 seconds of silence
Hold up, we say in unison
Our separate memories fresh in the way our voices turn
From conversational to revolutionary
You try again, and this is such a white-people thing to do
Give the story of how you may be white but
You were poor! You are white but not privileged!

1 or 3 infinite seconds of silence

ONE WAY BACK

On scabbed knees, fingers claw raw earth
Moonglow splinters seed the ground
Speaking in one language *tikha hiket ishtia*
Thieving hope as heavy as the
Fossilizing of hearts scattered across the grass
You slink and stutter
Spine bending to rainbow curve
Head near touching, almost there
As stone upon stone
Is placed on your back

Mouth now full of dirt.

WE ARE ALL FATED

Beneath the glacial planes of your cheekbones
Bring that slash of mouth

To my softest parts & thaw my soul
Floating in fairy dust as you

Take orders from the notes of swords
A residual conquering of what must be yours

Shielded by a singing sea
For dark thoughts & wicked deeds

Dancing around three wooden statues
The gods of days long buried

On ground once littered with heads
The seers and the hungry

Lusting for the same sustenance
From bone & blood & hope

Trail your tongue inside my thigh
For sails raise & wind haunts

TRUTH

She repeats: *you are a bull's-eye*
She waits, watching as I decide
You are a person who gets all the arrows
I'm a target, a human dartboard.

JUAN DIEGO'S ONE EYE

Beneath the dusty copper mountains
Forever secrets stretch across time zones and oceans
The fabric of whispers against pebble and weeds
All those deaths like fruit gone bad
Juan Diego, cracked lips and swollen-hearted, waited.

His place in history a bet against
Visions brought to life by discarded roses
For people love a saintly ghost story
A message of belief and future cannot
Be hidden by a thousand vultures.

Above the red hills, freckled with cacti
She arose, praying hands before silent mouth
Not singing, nor rejoicing; not crying, nor blaming
The mother of civilization opened arms for all peoples
A true mother, She of cinnamon skin, bowed head, rounded belly.

Juan Diego, peasant, man of no consequence until
Stared so hard, so long, his eyes became one
The Native and the Christian knit the broken backs of the people
With a miracle of sacrifice just in time
To blind the other eye.

SEWN TIGHT

Into the rocky ground by a thousand threaded needles piercing flesh and bone, veins tweaked like a harp and vibrating through the alphabet, whispered on repeat as only the steady force a, b, c, d, e, f will coax my heartbeat out of a narrowing throat tunnel carrying soiled air heavy with buzzing demons—naked and blue—leaving numbness in all left side extremities and a desire to cut off such offending limbs and give in, give up so the little blue fuckers can live inside me if it is their intention to give me crazy, make me crazy, go crazy beneath such unpredictable tug-o-war between reality and another reality because the thread becomes diamond forged and I'm sparkling with real fear, sweating, shivering, grasping for a breakthrough—a, b, c, d, e, f and fuck it all, resistance re-written.

COWBOYS & INDIAN PRINCESSES

Infestation of a homeland
Acrimonious Tonto speak
Not Native tongue, tied &
Served, zealotry, the main dish

Poca-haunt-us, we are calling you
Browned limbs & windblown hair
Embodiment of
Desire
Fear
Control
Body parts as trophies made into jewelry
We will wear your fingers around our waists

John Wayne, we are revealing you
Cocked hat & laconic musings
Illustration of
Showdown
Lawless
Power
Snakes slithering like loose ropes
We will wear your Americana around our necks

She is dangling now
Stuntwoman in a revisionist menu
Iconic beauty as memento
Token of erased history

He is searching now
Stuntman in an avenging diet
Epic western mascot
Lover of clandestine miscegenation

Pierced all together now
Arrow & Bullet

BOCA GRANDE
For Che

Just because you are qualified, doesn't mean you fit in
This fits the complaint of discrimination I am in the HR office to discuss
I say so, air quoting her, providing evidence
Not the first time I've heard something along these lines
Beginning with the muzzle I was threatened to receive for birthdays
To my amigos who shake their heads, *Filter!*
Not a compliment to my openness or communication skills
The repeated, *Sometimes I wish I hadn't raised you to be quite so vocal*
As if nature had nothing to do with it
The ex who in a heart-to-heart that turned red hot let me know: *You'd be the perfect woman…if you didn't have vocal cords*
The off the record telling of why I'd never be hired at a certain institution:
You are outspoken in your convictions, scaring people out of status quo, and these people don't hire people like you…they hire quieter women…it's just the way it is…unfortunately
I am living up to my childhood nickname, *Boca Grande*
And when I am silent…

THE RED DRESS FLATTENS ME

Did your fear and blood soak the soil, trickle
Through rocks to be cleansed and
Where did you go? Who took you there?
How many red dresses must we wear, and how long
As your face and stats, like a model's calling card
Yellow and tear from the sides of buildings, light poles
The dreams you had remain still because ones
Who love you cannot, will not, forget the gap
Of where you once held space
In a body that should have lasted,
Carried you into the years
Not into the hands of an epidemic
Recognizable by only those who have felt
The cutting away of, are left with the scars
And memories will never be enough
Or prayers or any medicine
To bring you back

ESCAPE GIRL BLUES

My roots, severed and bound years ago
Sprout and lace through my toes
Daring me to get up and just try to run
That mouth like you do—
All cobra-like, coy and coiled
Tongue pressed to teeth in feeble attempt
To thwart true nature, only nurtured
As I let go into the violet night
Nothing now can hide my voice
Not the music, nor laughter—so loud
Never in our manicured neighborhood
Nobody laughs hard without apologizing
Covering their mouths as if to push
The sound back in, retreat into the turtle shell of
Safety and a status quo I wasn't born
To practice and so the fight within continues
As my words red hot and unfiltered strike

My hand never comes close to my mouth

WOMEN BE WISE

There could be an apocalypse tomorrow
But probably not
To humor them, tell lies
With dry heart, dry mouth
Dehydrated as silence

When I get fucked, I never cry.

ADDITIONAL ACKNOWLEDGEMENTS

The following folks have championed my writing, and I owe you all many whiskeys (if appropriate): Daniel Barron, Sonrisa Barron, Elias Barron, Jengi, all the Mercer boys, Chennie, Christine Robbins, Carmen Hoover, Meagan MacVie, Grace Campbell, John Sibley-Williams, Sarah Vap, Cindy Stewart-Rinier, Jim Churchill-Dicks, Tod Marshall, Maya Jewell Zeller, Michael Schmeltzer, Samuel Ligon, Michael Albright, Nate Liederbach, Emily Van Kley, Marcus "Black Ceasar," Joan Banel, Elizabeth Stuckey-French, The Queens Peeps, T-B-Brown, Sarasoda, Andrew Wright, The Gray Skies Olympia posse, The Port Townsend Centrum folks, Hypatia—thank you for the residencies, all my Creative Writing and NWIC-Nisqually students, & Mosie: for *mi vida loca*, love you more.

www.ingramcontent.com/pod-product-compliance
Lightning Source LLC
LaVergne TN
LVHW041506070426
835507LV00012B/1366

Dawn Pichón Barron is a mixed-blood writer and educator. Her work has appeared or is forthcoming in *The Pittsburgh Poetry Review, Yellow Medicine Review, Washington 129 Anthology, Pontoon, Barrelhouse Blog, Of A Monstrous Child* (Lost Horse Press), and elsewhere. Currently she is the Director/Faculty of the Native Pathways Program at The Evergreen State College where she lives at the southern tip of the Salish Sea. She can be reached @pigeongirlsgot.